espe
Dads

by robert j. strand

ORDERING INFORMATION

Individual sales can be had at selected bookstores or you can order direct from Rojon, Inc. at P. O. Box 3898, Springfield, MO 65808-3898 or call our customer service number, 1-888-389-0225.

Quantity sales are available at special discounts, bulk purchases or case lots by corporations, associations, churches and others. For details, contact Rojon, Inc. at the above address.

Orders by trade bookstores and wholesalers can be made through the above address as well.

ISBN: 0-9717039-3-0

Second Printing: January 2006

All Scripture references are from The New King James Version (Thomas Nelson Publishers) unless otherwise noted.

You can also make contact at the above address for speaking engagements, writers' seminars, keynote addresses or other books by the writer, Robert J. Strand.

ROJON PUBLISHING
P.O. Box 3898
Springfield, MO 65808-3898

Design and layout by Marc McBride

Presented to: _____

Presented by: _____

Date: _____

DEDICATION:

To all the fathers who are involved in the world's most exciting and underrated task of raising little ones to become responsible citizens and productive contributors in today's world! Further... as you give fatherly love, which is a miraculous substance which God multiplies as it's divided, know that your sacrifices will live on in the coming generations!
BLESSINGS!

CONTENTS

THE STORY OF TAPS

Reportedly, it all began in 1862 during the Civil War, when Union Army Captain Robert Ellicombe was with his men near Harrison's Landing in Virginia.

The Confederate Army was on the north side of a narrow strip of land over which the battle raged. During the night, Captain Ellicombe heard the agonizing moans of a soldier who was apparently severely wounded and who had been left on the field of battle. Not knowing if this soldier was Union or Confederate, the Captain decided to risk his life and bring the fallen man back to his own lines for medical attention.

Carefully, deliberately, slowly, crawling on his stomach through the sporadic gun fire, the Captain reached the wounded soldier and began dragging him back to friendly lines, toward his own camp, to the field hospital. When the Captain finally reached his lines, he discovered it was a Confederate soldier... now dead. The Captain lit a lantern to check out this enemy further. Suddenly, he caught his breath and went numb with shock. In the dim light he made out the face of the soldier. It was that of his own son!

The boy had been studying music in a Southern college when the war broke out. Without telling his parents, he had enlisted in the Confederate Army.

The following morning, heartbroken, grief stricken, the father asked permission of his superior officer to give his son a full military funeral and burial despite his enemy status. His request was only partially granted. The Captain then asked if he could have a group of Union Army band members play a funeral dirge for his son at the burial. The request was denied since the soldier was a Confederate. However... out of respect for the grieving father, he could choose a single, lone musician to play.

The Captain chose a bugler. He asked the bugler to play a series of musical notes he had found on a piece of paper in the pocket of his son's uniform. This wish was granted.

The haunting melody we now know as "Taps" was played for the first time. And... became a tradition you still hear at military funerals today.

Okay...
Parents who have fine children usually have children who have fine parents!

I will be to Him a Father, And He shall be to Me a Son.
(Hebrews 1:5b)

"I don't think we're going to get out of this thing. I'm going to have to go out on faith," so said the voice of Todd Beamer, passenger, who said "Let's roll" as he led the charge against the terrorists on United Flight 93. That's the plane that crashed in the Pennsylvania countryside. The whole world knows how brave Beamer and his fellow passengers were on September 11.

Later, in an article titled "The Real Story of Flight 93" which appeared in *Newsweek* we learned more fully what had buttressed that bravery: his faith in Jesus Christ. Todd died as he lived, a faithful, born again believer. The gripping details were taken from the recovered cockpit voice recorder. "Todd had been afraid," *Newsweek* related. "More than once, he cried out for his Savior."

After the passengers were herded to the back of the jet, Beamer called the GTE Customer Center in Oakbrook, Illinois. He told supervisor Lisa Jefferson about the hijacking. "The passengers were planning to jump the terrorists," he said and asked her to pray with him. The article relates, "Beamer kept a Lord's Prayer bookmark in his Tom Clancy novel, but he didn't need any prompting. He began to recite the ancient litany, and Jefferson joined him: "Our Father which art in heaven, hallowed be thy name..." When they finished, Beamer added: "Jesus, help me!"

And then, Beamer and fellow passengers prayed this same prayer that has comforted millions down through the centuries. It's the prayer David wrote in a time of anguish: "The Lord is my shepherd, I shall not want... Yea, though I walk through the valley of the shadow of death, I will fear no evil..."

Then came those famous last words: "Are you guys ready? LET'S ROLL!"

We now know from the cockpit voice recorder that Beamer and other passengers wrestled with the hijackers and forced the plane to crash into the ground, killing themselves and the hijackers. This foiled what was believed to have been the hijackers' plan to fly Flight 93 into the Capitol or White House.

As Flight 93 hurtled towards destruction, Todd could not have known that his quiet prayer and act of bravery would ultimately be heard by millions. That the story of his last acts on earth would be a witness to his faith in the Lord Jesus Christ, whom he loved and served to his death!

Forgiveness

"You know, in the Lord's Prayer, it asks us to forgive our trespasses as we forgive those who trespass against us.
As Todd prayed this prayer in the last moments of his life, in a way, he was forgiving those people for what they were doing, the most horrible thing you could ever do to someone."

Lisa Beamer, NBC Dateline interview

You prepare a table before me in the presence of my enemies, You anoint my head with oil; My cup runs over. Surely goodness and mercy shall follow me All the days of my life; And I will dwell in the house of the LORD Forever. (Psalm 23:5-6)

SURVIVAL RATES

While the subject of 9/11 is still on our minds, let's take a look at the other side of the numbers which came out of New York, Washington and Pennsylvania. These were deplorable acts which we must never forget but there is a somewhat uplifting side that the mainstream media has not reported... the survival rates and some positive news about the attacks. Let's look at the buildings and the planes.

The World Trade Center: These twin towers of the Trade Center were places of employment for more than 50,000 people. With the "Missing List" at just over 3,000 that means about 94% of the targeted people survived the attack. A 90% on a test is an "A."

The Pentagon: Some 23,000 people were the target of a third plane aimed at the Pentagon. The latest count shows 123 lost their lives. This is an amazing 99.5% survival rate. In addition, the plane seems to have come in too low, too early, to affect a large portion of the building. And, the section which was hit was the first of five sections to undergo renovations that would help protect the Pentagon from terrorist attacks. It had recently completed straightening and blast-proofing, saving more lives. This attack was vicious and sad, but a statistical failure.

American Airlines Flight 77: This Boeing 757 flown into the outside of the Pentagon could have carried up to 289 people, yet only 64 were aboard. Luckily 78% of the seats were empty.

American Airlines Flight 11: This Boeing 767 could have held up to 351 people, but only carried 92. Thankfully 74% of the seats were unfilled.

United Airlines Flight 175: Another Boeing 767 that could have seated 351 people only had 65 people on board. Fortunately it was 81% empty.

United Airlines Flight 93: This Boeing 757 is one of the most uplifting stories yet. The smallest flight to be hijacked with only 45 people aboard out of a possible 289 had 84% of its capacity unused. Yet these people stood up to the attackers and thwarted a fourth attempted destruction of a national landmark, saving untold numbers of lives in the process.

Out of potentially 74,280 Americans directly targeted by these cowards, 94% survived or avoided the attacks. That's a higher survival rate than heart attacks, breast cancer, kidney transplants and liver transplants... all survivable sicknesses.

The hijacked planes were nearly empty, the Pentagon was hit at its strongest point, the overwhelming majority of people in the World Trade Center buildings escaped and thankfully, only a handful of passengers gave the ultimate sacrifice to save even more lives.

Today's Thought

We don't need to live in fear of the terrorists... the odds are against them in more ways than they could know.

He who dwells in the secret place of the Most High shall abide under the shadow of the Almighty. I will say of the Lord, "He is my refuge and my fortress; My God, in Him I will trust."
(Psalm 91:1-2)

The tell-tale "green and yellow" Zip-Lock seals on your air bags.
Ralph Nader's home phone number is written on the dashboard.
The hood ornament is an ostrich with its head in the sand.
"Jaws of Life" are in the trunk.
Turn on the wipers and guys climb out of the trunk with squeegees.
It was disqualified from the Soap Box Derby for lack of structural integrity.
The car has spent more time on "60 Minutes" than on the road.
Oil spills on your driveway prompt a visit from Greenpeace.
Changing the preset radio stations voids the car's warranty.
Two words: "Pontiac Sunkist."
Passenger side "airbag" is actually Rush Limbaugh in the glove box.
Manufactured in Zchkynk, Crzyktjkystan.

Then... there is the list of the "Worst Cars of the Millennium" as voted for on NPR's "Car Talk" and described by previous owners:

The Yugo: "At least it had heated rear windows so your hands could stay warm while you pushed."

Daihatsu Charade: "It was as if Daihatsu took aluminum foil and shaped it into a car."

Ford Pinto: "Remember that great Pinto bumper sticker? 'Hit me and we blow up together'!"

American Motors Gremlin: "It was entirely possible to read an entire Russian novel during the pause between stepping on the gas and feeling any semblance of forward motion."

Renault Le Car: "It would put you in mortal danger if you had an accident with anything larger than a croissant."

Volkswagen Bus: "There was no heat... unless, that is, the auxiliary gas heater caught fire."

Cadillac Cimarron: "When we traded it in, my wife was upset because we didn't keep it long enough for her to buy a gun and shoot it."

Fiat X1/9: "It ran fine... that is, unless it was too wet, too cold, too hot or too dark outside."

Chevrolet Vega: "As far as I could tell, the car was built from compressed rust."

Oh, well... this is a guy thing and no one else will understand the whys and where-fores.

Today's Thought

We had complete confidence in reaching the moon. Now if we could only feel the same way about getting across town.

Some trust in chariots, and some in horses; But we will remember the name of the LORD our God. (Psalm 20:7)

A JESUS LANDING

Howard County, Indiana Sheriff Jerry Marr got a disturbing call one Saturday afternoon. His six-year-old grandson, Mikey, had been hit by a car while fishing with his dad. The father and son were near a bridge by the Kokomo Reservoir when a woman lost control of her car, slid off the embankment and hit Mikey at about fifty miles an hour. Sheriff Marr had seen the results of such accidents and feared the worst. When he got to St. Joseph Hospital, he rushed to the emergency room to find Mikey conscious and in fairly good spirits.

"Mikey, what happened?" the Sheriff asked.

"Well, Papaw," replied Mikey, "I was fishin' with Dad and some lady runned me over; I flew into a mud puddle and broke my fishin' pole and I didn't get to catch no fish!"

As it turned out, the impact propelled Mikey about 200 feet, over a few trees, an embankment and into the middle of a mud puddle. His only injuries were to his right femur bone which had broken in two places. Mikey had surgery to place pins in his leg; Otherwise he was fine.

Since all he could talk about was his broken fishing pole, the Sheriff went to Wal-Mart and bought Mikey a new one while he was in surgery so he could have it when he came out. The next day the Sheriff sat with Mikey to keep him company in the hospital.

Mikey was enjoying his new fishing pole and talking about when he could go fishing again as he practiced casting into the trash can. When they were alone, Mikey, matter-of-factly, said, "Pawpaw, did you know Jesus is real?"

"Well," the Sheriff replied a bit startled, "Yes, Jesus is real to all who believe in

Him and love Him in their hearts."

"No," said Mikey. "I mean Jesus is REALLY real!"

"What do you mean?" asked the Sheriff.

"I know He's real 'cause I saw Him," said Mikey, still casting into the trash can.

"You did?" asked the Sheriff.

"Yep," replied Mikey. "When that lady runned me over and broke my fishing pole, Jesus caught me in His arms and laid me down in the mud puddle."

Uniting Men & Meaning, the magazine of United Methodist Men, Vol. 5, #3, 2002

A Constant

"The angels are the dispensers and administrators of the divine beneficence toward us; they regard our safety, undertake our defense, direct our ways and exercise a constant solicitude that no evil befall us."

John Calvin

For He shall give His angels charge over you,
To keep you in all your ways. In their hands they shall bear you
up, Lest you dash your foot against a stone. (Psalm 91:11, 12)

BUZZARD, BAT, BUMBLEBEE

If you put a buzzard in a pen that is six feet by eight feet and open at the top, the bird, in spite of its ability to fly, will be an absolute prisoner. The reason is that a buzzard always begins a flight from the ground with a run of ten to twelve feet. Without space to run, as is its habit, it will not even attempt to fly but will remain a prisoner for life in a small jail with no top.

The ordinary bat that flies at night and happens to be a remarkably nimble, fabulous flying creature in the air, cannot take off from a level place. If it is placed on the floor or flat ground, all it can do is shuffle about helplessly and, no doubt, painfully, until it reaches some slight elevation from which it can launch itself into the air. Then it can take off.

A bumblebee, if dropped into an open glass tumbler, will remain there until it dies, unless it is released. It never sees the means of escape at the top, but persists in trying to find some way out through the sides near the bottom. It will attempt to find a way out where none exists until it destroys itself.

In many ways, there are lots of people like the buzzard, the bat and the bumblebee. They are struggling about with all their problems and frustrations without the realization that the answer is right there... ABOVE them!

Dad... it's not a sign of weakness to seek for Divine help from above. In fact, it's a point of strength. And as you do seek for Divine help and guidance, make sure that your children learn that lesson from you and your lifestyle.

STICK WITH THE STUFF

Lee, a godly man, church leader, community leader and father
tells his story of learning the value of sticking with it. As a teen in "Industrial Shop" class he chose as his project the building of a farm feed wagon. It tested his zeal. He started out great... about a third of the way to completion, the job was too big. It beat him down... he knew he'd never finish it.

But his teacher encouraged him and he didn't give up. Morning by morning, day by day, even in after school hours, he managed to complete it by the end of school. His perseverance was rewarded by the satisfaction of a job well done.

The story doesn't end there. Lee grew, married and began farming on his own. He had three boys. Life was good. It was harvest time and the hired man and the two oldest boys were auguring corn into the wooden corn crib. The boys were up on top playing on the dividers. Both had been warned of the danger of flowing corn. The downward suction of flowing corn is strong enough to pull a full-grown man under. Yet, for some reason the oldest boy jumped into the corn... he was caught. The younger brother jumped in to help and was caught, too. Both screamed for help!

Fortunately the hired man heard their yells. He shut off the auger and hollered for Lee.

Running to the bins... a farmer's nightmare assaulted Lee. Fear ripped at his heart and panic seized his mind. The boys had been caught in the flow of grain. They were buried alive and didn't have much time. Lee grabbed a claw hammer and pounded on the side of the wooden bin with all his might. The hammer bounced back like a rubber ball. The blow was like hitting a granite rock. Lee's heart sank. His boys were suffocating, he was done.

Then...in his own words, he remembered the school project. The lesson from his youth kicked in. He scoured around and found a piece of 4 x 4 and attacked the side of the bin. With all the desire of a father's love he pounded on the resistant wall. Under this tenacious battering the wooden siding splintered apart, releasing a wall of yellow corn and two struggling boys. They were scared and one had started to turn blue...but they recovered!

Now... the Question

Dad, have you been wondering, "What's the use?" The task you're facing appears too big, you are too tired, the situation is impossible.

Lee will tell you otherwise.

Not giving up and staying with the stuff saved his children.

Don't give up, don't give in, because you can make a difference when you don't quit!

He Himself has said, "I will never leave you nor forsake you."
So we may boldly say: "The LORD is my helper;
I will not fear, What can man do to me?" (Hebrews 13:5b-6)

THE FATHER'S FACE

This is a poignant story of a young husband whose wife died and left him with a small son. Back home, after the funeral, with all the guests and family members gone... they went to bed as soon as it was dark. Why? Because the grieving husband could think of nothing else he wanted to do in this time of sorrow.

They both lay in the darkness, numb with hurt and sorrow. Soon, the little boy broke the stillness from his bedroom with disturbing questions: "Daddy, where is Mommy?" "Why did she have to leave us?" "What will happen to her, now?" The father attempted to get him to sleep but the questions kept coming from his sad, childish mind.

Finally, the father got up, went to his child's bedroom, picked up his son and brought him back into bed with him. But the child was still disturbed and restless and continued to ask probing, heartbreaking questions. Questions that really didn't have answers. The father attempted to calm and comfort him.

Then, the youngster reached a little hand through the darkness, placed it on his father's face and asked, "Daddy, is your face toward me?"

Given assurance, verbally and by his own touch, that his father's face was looking in his direction, the boy then softly said, through his sobs,

"If your face is looking at me, I think I can go to sleep."

Dad… you can count on it! The Heavenly Father's face is always toward us.

Today's Quote

Man is harder than iron, stronger than stone and more fragile than a rose.

Turkish Proverb

As a father pities his children, So the LORD pities those who fear Him. For He knows our frame; He remembers that we are dust. (Psalm 103:13-14)

A STORY WITH A KICK

The Orlando Predators of the AFL (Arena Football League) desperately needed a kicker and got a great recommendation from Miami Dolphins kicking coach, Doug Blevins, about a prospect named Nick Gatto out of Arkansas State. Blevins said he was good enough to kick in the NFL but lacked pro experience. He failed to mention one thing… Gatto, 24, was born with a right arm that stops at the elbow.

When he failed to get drafted, Gatto sent homemade video highlights to every NFL and AFL team. In the meantime he spent the year working with at-risk-teenagers as a substitute teacher back home in Spring, Texas.

"Nick is a very inspirational person," Blevins says, who began working with Gatto to improve his kicking skills. "Beyond that, he's a good kicker."

When you have grown up being teased mercilessly as a child there are reactions to deal with. Nick himself described his arrival in Orlando on the AFL scene like this: "The first reaction is 'Who is this guy?' Then when they see me kick, they start going, 'Holy cow!' The coaches already know that I can kick. And so when I do show up, well then, they see who I really am. So then they're like, 'OK, that's who he is. He can kick. So he's like everybody else." Gatto signed for the AFL minimum per game and was pumped.

Jay Gruden, coach of the Predators, whose brother is Jon Gruden of the Tampa Bay Buccaneers, could only smile when Gatto eagerly got into some tackles after his first few kicks. His longest kick for Orlando was a 47-yard field goal.

Gatto's father, Sal, says: "He's almost fulfilled his dream. He's been talking about playing in the NFL ever since he was young." The 5-11, 188-pound Gatto also played football, basketball, baseball and ran track in high school. He can also bench press 335 pounds… he uses both arms, balancing the bar slightly unevenly, and has been timed at under 4.4 seconds in the 40-yard dash.

When Gatto would come home crying after being teased about his arm as a boy, he'd ask his mother why he was born that way. "She'd say, 'God has made you for a very special reason. And when the time is right, then He is going to show that to you.' So I go on. And that's what I say to myself each and every day. God has put me here for a reason. And each and every day He is showing that to me."

Gatto's dad says things improved once he entered high school. The teasing stopped and others treated him fairly. He also developed a way to make people comfortable about his arm. He is still working through a speech impediment.

His attitude is best described by former Arkansas State special teams coach Don Yanowsky, "Nick's attitude is so great that he should be a walking billboard for "the glass is half-full!"

Both Nick and his dad chuckled when retold this remark. Only their family knows how tough it was at times for Gatto to have come this far. Dad and son talk about "a lot of sweat and tears."

Opportunity
That has been my dream, each and every day, me saying,
"All I want is one opportunity, and that opportunity is here!"

Nick Gatto

I will praise You, for I am fearfully and wonderfully made;
Marvelous are Your works, And that my soul knows very well.
(Psalm 139:14)

101 WAYS TO PRAISE OR ENCOURAGE A CHILD

When sharing blessings, acceptance or praise... it doesn't necessarily have to be a special occasion. Do it and do it often. Let these things become important in your thinking and vocabulary. Give it as a response even when a child least expects it. Too many children go through life seeking for approval... don't withhold it when it is in your power to speak it! Here they are:

WOW... Way to go... Super... You're special... Outstanding... Excellent... Great... Good... Neat... Well done... Remarkable... I knew you could do it... I'm proud of you... Fantastic... Super star... Nice work... Looking good... You're on top of it... Beautiful... Now you're flying... You're catching on... Now you've got it... You're incredible... Bravo... You're fantastic... Hurray for you... You're on target... You're on your way... How nice... How smart... Good job... That's incredible... Hot dog... Dynamite... You're beautiful... You're unique... Nothing can stop you now... Good for you... I like you... You're a winner... Remarkable job... Beautiful work... Spectacular... You're spectacular... You're darling... You're precious... Great discovery... You've discovered the secret... You figured it out... Fantastic job... Hip, hip, hurray... Bingo... Magnificent... Marvelous... Terrific... You're important... Phenomenal... You're sensational... Super work... Creative work... Super job... Fantastic job... Exceptional performance... You're a real trooper... You are responsible... You are exciting... You learned it right... What an imagination... What a good listener... You are fun... You're growing up... You tried hard... You care... Beautiful sharing... Outstanding performance... You're a good friend... I trust you... You're important... You mean a lot to me... You make me happy... You belong... You've got a friend ... You make me laugh... You brighten my day... I respect you... You mean the world to me... That's correct... You're a joy... You're a treasure... You're wonderful...

You're perfect... Awesome... A+ job... You're a-okay... My buddy... You made my day... That's the best... A big hug... A big kiss... I LOVE YOU!!

Compliments, Charter Hospital of Sioux Falls, South Dakota

And always remember: A smile is an unspoken blessing that is worth a thousand words It's even more powerful when you combine a smile with a word of encouragement, a word of praise, or a word of blessing.

JUST DO IT!!

Dad, you no longer have an excuse because you can't find the right words at the right moment. Perhaps you are thinking: "My parents never blessed me with these kinds of words in this way." Or... it's possible that you may have been a victim of neglect and because of it you are making your own children victims of your neglect and hurt. I challenge you to break this cycle of silence! Begin today sharing acceptance and blessing! And one more word. No, you can't do it too much if you are consistent so your children know it is meaningful and comes honestly.

Just do it!

You, too, will be blessed and will have become a blessing!

This is the way you shall bless the children...Say to them: "The LORD bless you and keep you; The LORD make His face shine upon you, And be gracious to you; The LORD lift up His countenance upon you, And give you peace. (Numbers 6:23b-26)

SOME SPORTS SHORT SHOTS

• Former New Orleans Saints running back George Rogers when asked about an upcoming season: "I want to rush for 1,500 or 1,000 yards, whichever comes first."

• Bill Peterson, a Florida State football coach: "You guys line up alphabetically by height." And another one by Bill: "You guys pair up in groups of three, then lineup in a circle."

• Shaquille O'Neal on whether he had visited the Parthenon during his visit to Greece: "I can't really remember the names of the clubs that we went to." How about one more by Shaq: "I've won at every level, except college and pro."

• Chuck Nevitt, 1982, North Carolina State basketball player, explaining to Coach Valvano why he appeared nervous at practice: "My sister's expecting a baby, and I don't know if I'm going to be an uncle or an aunt."

• Arnold Palmer: "I have a tip that can take five strokes off anyone's golf game. It is called an eraser."

• Steve Spurrier, in 1991, then coach of Florida U. football, on a fire at Auburn's football dorm which had destroyed twenty books: "But the real tragedy was that fifteen of them hadn't been colored yet."

• Shelby Metcalf, basketball coach at Texas A & M, recounting what he told a player who received four Fs and one D: "Son, looks to me like you're spending too much time on one subject."

• Mickey Mantle: "He who has the fastest golf cart never has a bad lie."

During a tournament basketball game, a coach called a time out and singled out one of his players, the starting point guard. He asked the young man, "Do you know the meaning of cooperation?"

This young boy answered, "Sure coach, I know what cooperation is."

The coach then asked, "Do you know the meaning of teamwork?"

The point guard answered, "Yes, I know what teamwork is."

The coach continued, "Do you know what fairness means?"

The young man answered, "Yes, coach, I know what fairness means."

The coach went on, "Do you know what self control means?"

The player replied, "Yes, coach, I know what self control means."

The coach continued the quiz, "Do you know what balance means?"

The player, a bit puzzled, replied, "Yes, coach I know."

The coach asked, "Do you know what magnanimous means?"

Again, the player answered, "Yes, coach, I think I know what magnanimous means."

And finally, the coach asked, "And do you know what good sportsmanship is?"

"Yes, coach," the boy responded, "I know what good sportsmanship is. It's when a call does not go our way, but we accept it and keep playing. We don't get angry or say mean things or swear at the ref."

"That's right," said the coach. "Now will you go to the bleachers where your parents are sitting and explain to your dad what you already know?!"

How You Played

For when the One Great Scorer comes,
To write against your name,
He writes, not that you won or lost,
But how you played the game.

Grantland Rice

*I have fought the good fight, I have finished the race,
I have kept the faith. (II Timothy 4:7)*

Would you agree with me? Life's three big questions are:

(1) Where did I come from? (2) Why am I here? (3) Where am I going? Agree? Maybe not, but let's go a bit further.

Consider this... true success in life is achieving the purposes for which God created us. Only then will we find true happiness and fulfillment. God guarantees success to anyone who will take the time to meditate and think on His Word on a consistent basis.

Let's go at this from another perspective. Ask yourself these questions:

1. How can I make a difference?

2. What skills can I build on to develop my career?

3. How can I find meaning in life?

4. What is the best way I can contribute?

5. In what can I best excel?

6. What obstacles can I overcome and use my knowledge to help others?

7. What kind of legacy do I want to leave?

8. How may I receive eternal life?

9. What am I willing to sacrifice in the short term in order to develop my long-term purpose?

10. What is the payoff for staying true to my purpose?

11. What possible recognition might I be able to receive?
12. Why is developing purpose important to me?

Questions by Jim Bickford, American Dreams

Transforming Leaders

I am personally convinced that one person can be a change catalyst, a "transformer" in any situation.

It requires vision, initiative, patience, respect, persistence, courage and faith to be a transforming leader.

Stephen R. Covey

Not that I have already attained, or am already perfected;
but I press on... I do not count myself to have apprehended;
But one thing I do, Forgetting those things which are behind and
reaching forward to those which are ahead, I press toward the
goal for the prize... (Philippians 3:12-14)

DID I EVER TELL HIM?

The overwhelming grief of a father who mourned the loss of his son is depicted in the life story movie "8 Seconds." This movie takes its name from the time required to make a successful bull ride, yes, it's only eight seconds but can seem like an eternity. The scene takes place when the father of bull rider, Lane Frost, sits alone in a dark room in obvious mental anguish and grief.

His son was the world champion bull rider Lane Frost who had been killed while riding a bull in Cheyenne, Wyoming. Lane's mother walks into the room, comes up behind him and as she listens he begins to pour out his heart of sorrow with these poignant words:

"I've been sittin' here tryin' to remember if I ever told him. I told him I was proud of him. That he did a good job. But I can't remember a single time I told him I loved him."

Dad... don't forget to say it while you can and have the opportunity!

Why is it so hard for some dads to say these simple words, "I love you?" An expression of love from a father is as necessary as it is from a mother. Perhaps you were raised by parents who were not given to such expressions. Or, it might have been that it was taken for granted in your growing-up-home but never put into words. Children crave for expressions of love and acceptance and we should not assume they know they are loved. Remove all doubt and say it! Say it often and make sure that your actions which follow also are consistent acts of love.

Dad...say it! Just do it!

Good Replaces Bad

"Returning violence for violence only multiplies violence, adding deeper darkness to a night already devoid of stars.
Darkness cannot drive out darkness; only light can do that.
Hate cannot drive out hate;
Only love can do that."

Dr. Martin Luther King, Jr.

Love suffers long and is kind; love does not envy; love does not parade itself, is not puffed up; does not behave rudely, does not seek its own, is not provoked, thinks no evil... bears all things, believes all things, hopes all things, endures all things.
Love never fails! (I Corinthians 13:4-8)

NO TIME FOR TAUNTING

An atheistic professor was teaching a college science class. He began the class by telling them there was no empirical evidence for God and he was going to prove that there was not a God. He lifted his face toward the ceiling and taunted, "God, if you are an actual being, then I want you to knock me off this platform. You have fifteen minutes to prove yourself!"

Every couple of minutes the atheist professor would repeat his taunt, "Here I am God, I'm still waiting." He increased his taunt by saying, "Okay, God, maybe you're just too busy. Perhaps you could send just one of your angels or one of your messengers instead!"

This professor was down to the last two minutes when the star football player happened to be walking past the classroom and overheard the tauntings of the professor. This huge football player walked into the classroom and tackled the professor full force and sent him flying off the platform!

The professor managed to pick himself up and was obviously shaken. He turned to the football player and asked, "Where did you come from and how come you knocked me off the platform?"

The football player replied, "God was too busy to mess with your nonsense, so I guess He sent me instead!"

Okay

You never find atheists in foxholes, in burning houses, running from tornadoes, trapped in a wrecked car or in a plane that is about to crash.

The fool has said in his heart, "There is no God." They are corrupt, They have done abominable works, There is none who does good. (Psalm 14:1)

NOT IN THE KISS

A six-year-old girl went up to her daddy who was very busy at work on his computer, completing a job that was to be handed in first thing in the morning. He was so busy and focused that he didn't notice her for a while. She moved a bit closer and into his line of sight until he finally noticed her. He said, "Honey, what do you want?"

She said, "Daddy, it's my bedtime. Mommy said if I came and stood beside you, you'd give me a hug and good-night kiss."

"All right," he said. He gave her a hug and kiss and said, "Okay, now off to bed you go."

He went back to his computer because he had this important report due the next morning. He was totally absorbed in his work.

About ten minutes later... he looked up from the monitor and his daughter was standing there again. He said, "Honey, I gave you your hug and kiss. Now, what more do you want?"

She said, "Daddy, you gave me the hug and kiss but you weren't in it. So you need to do it again."

Kids... aren't they great? But, oh so honest!

This is just another reminder that our time with little ones goes quickly by and the opportunities for hugs and kisses may also be over too soon. To be a father is more than doing it biologically... it's being there emotionally when you are with them physically. It's so easy to let the urgent things of life push out the important, long-term things.

Remembering

Children will soon forget your presents... but they will always remember your presence!

Children, obey your parents in the Lord, this is right. Honor your father and mother, which is the first commandment with promise: that it may be well with you and you may live long on the earth. And you fathers, do not provoke your children to wrath, but bring them up in the training and admonition of the Lord. (Ephesians 6:1-4)

Do you remember the story of Moses leading the children of Israel out of Egyptian bondage? Exciting reading... but what was Moses to do with them once they arrived in the wilderness desert? They had to be fed and fed is what happened. But there's more to the story.

According to the Quartermaster General of the Army, it is reported that Moses would have needed about 1,500 tons of food each day to feed them. In order to ship that much food every day two freight trains, each a mile long, would be required!

Besides, you must remember, they were out in the desert so they would need to have firewood to cook their food. This would take approximately 4,000 tons of wood and a few more freight trains, each a mile long to deliver it on a daily basis. Think... they were forty years in transit!

And, oh, yes, they would need water. If they had only enough to drink and wash a few dishes and take a weekly sponge bath, it would take some 11,000,000 gallons per day. And another freight train with tanker cars miles long just to bring their daily water!

Another consideration... they had to cross the Red Sea in a short period of time because of their pursuers. Now if they went on a narrow path, double file, the line would stretch about 800 miles long and would require 35 days and nights to get them all across. So, apparently, there had to be a dry-land crossing about three miles wide so they could walk 5,000 abreast to get them all over in a single night!

How about another problem? Each time they set up camp at day's end, they required a camp ground covering a number of square miles. Remember, they had no high-rise tents so they all needed space. It's estimated it could have covered about ten to twelve square miles. And we haven't even touched on the need for shoes or clothing, or sanitation, or medical services, or heating and cooling. Think, we haven't covered the fact that these needs went on for forty long years!

Do you think Moses figured all this out before he left Egypt with some estimated three to four million folks? I think not!

How was it accomplished? Moses believed in his God and God took care of these things for him and his people.

Now the big question: DO YOU THINK GOD HAS ANY PROBLEM TAKING CARE OF YOU AND YOUR FAMILY'S NEEDS?

Remember

God's love is always with you, His promises are true,
And we give Him all our cares and concerns,
You can be assured that He will see you through!
So, Dad, when the road you're traveling on seems difficult at best, just remember to believe and pray,
And let God do the rest!

And my God shall supply all your need according to His riches in glory by Christ Jesus! (Philippians 4:19)

CAN I BORROW TEN DOLLARS?

He came home from work late again, tired and irritated to find his five-year-old son waiting for him at the door. "Daddy, may I ask you a question?"

"Sure son, what is it?" replied the man.

"Daddy, how much money do you make an hour?"

"That's really none of your business. What makes you ask such a question?" the man responded with a bit of irritation.

"I just want to know. Please tell me," pleaded the boy.

"If you must know," the father replied, "about $25 an hour."

"Oh," the little guy looked up and asked, "Daddy, may I please borrow ten dollars?"

The dad was irritated, "If the only reason you wanted to know how much money I make is just so you can borrow some to buy a silly toy or other nonsense, march yourself off to bed. Think about why you're being so selfish. I work long and hard to provide for you and don't have time for such childish games." The little boy quietly went to his room and shut the door.

The man sat down with the paper and was more irritated about his son's questioning. Later, about an hour or so, he had calmed down and thought perhaps there was a real need for the ten dollars. He went to his son's bedroom and quietly opened the door. "Are you asleep, son?"

"No, Daddy, I'm still awake," replied the five-year-old.

"I've been thinking, maybe I was too hard on you," said this dad. "It's been a long day and I took out my aggravation on you. Here's the ten dollars you asked for."

The little boy sat up, beaming. "Oh, thank you Daddy!" he yelled. Then reaching under his pillow, he pulled out some more crumpled bills. The man, since the son already had money, started to get irritated again. His son slowly counted out his money and then looked up at his dad.

"Why did you want more money if you already had some?" the father grumbled.

"Because I didn't have enough, but now I do," the little guy replied. "Daddy, I have twenty-five dollars now. Can I buy one hour of your time?"

Think About It

"The family is not one of several alternative lifestyles; it is not an arena in which rights are negotiated; it is not an old-fashioned barrier to a promiscuous sex life; it is not a set of cost-benefit calculations.

It is a commitment for which there is no feasible substitute. No child ought to be brought into a world where that commitment... from both parents... is absent."

James Q. Wilson

As for Me, behold, My covenant is with you, and you shall be a father of many...
(Genesis 17:4)

This supposedly is a true story… but then again, it has almost attained the status of an "urban" legend. Well, anyway, it's fun.

Mickey Mantle, Hall of Fame baseball player had a friend who was more than happy to let him hunt on his Texas ranch. One day, he took his teammate, Billy Martin, along for a hunt on the ranch. Billy stayed in the car while Mickey checked with his friend if it would be okay.

Mickey was happily given permission to hunt along with Billy… but the rancher asked for a favor. His old mule was going blind and had become crippled but because he was a favorite pet, he just didn't have the heart to put him out of his misery. So he asked Mickey if he would shoot the old mule as a favor.

When Mickey got back to the car, he decided to play a trick on Billy and pretended to be angry. "What's wrong?" asked Billy.

"My good friend told me NO HUNTING!!!" Mickey pounded his fist on the dashboard pretending anger and said, "That guy, who is my good friend, made me so mad I'm going into that corral and I'm going to shoot one of his mules!" With that, Mickey jumped out of the car and headed to the corral with his gun. In quick order he took care of the mule and started back to the car to tell his friend it was all a big joke. At that moment, Mickey heard two shots fired and came around the car to find Billy Martin standing over two dead cows! "What are you doing?" asked Mickey!

Martin answered, "I just saw how mad you were and I wanted to let the rancher know he couldn't fool with me, either!"

Anger Management

Average percentage increase in a wife's blood pressure during an argument with her husband: SIX.

Average percentage increase in a husband's blood pressure during an argument with his wife: FOURTEEN!

Therefore, a husband needs forgiveness more than a wife but he also needs to forgive more than a wife does, in the need for better heart-health.

Be angry, and do not sin:
Do not let the sun go down on your wrath, nor give place
to the devil. (Ephesians 4:26)

George and Nellie Balisky of Peace River, Alberta, Canada, may have set a record in raising six missionary children, plus four more who are active Christians at home and help support the family's "overseas branch."

Four of the Balisky kids serve with the Sudan Interior Mission (SIM) in Africa. A daughter is with the Central American Mission in Honduras. And a son, a physician, is with the Overseas Missionary Fellowship in Thailand.

Recently, SIM asked the Balisky's oldest son, Ralph, who supervises a missionary boys home and farm in Nigeria, to recount some of his parents' doings that resulted in such outstanding children.

He noted: "Mother and Dad gave us all to the Lord before we were born. Though Dad's application to the Moody Bible Institute was rejected because of his fourth grade education, he and mother dedicated themselves to raising a Christian family.

"We had family prayers every day. We didn't always like it when Dad said that everyone would pray, right around the circle. But it did something to us that I can't explain.

"Dad was our friend and we loved him. But he wasn't a buddy… he was our father. And he was the head of the family. There was no court of appeal above Dad! Our parents were always fair to us and we wouldn't be punished unless we deserved it. But we never got away with anything either.

"Our parents were committed Christian stewards. Each year they made a mission promise, even when they didn't know where the money would come from.

"They never pressured us to become missionaries; they insisted we get guidance from God. But it was no secret that they would be very happy if some of us did become missionaries.

"They lived the way they talked. They set high ideals before us. And they loved us."

Now... how's that for a formula for raising special children? I count at least six steps and concepts that could very well serve as a parenting pattern to follow... if you would like to raise caring, giving kids.

Today's Thought

You and I have the gospel because missionaries have come our way at sometime in the past.

Oh, sing to the Lord a new song! Sing to the Lord, all the earth. Sing to the Lord, bless His name; Proclaim the good news of His salvation from day to day. Declare His glory among the nations, His wonders among all peoples.
(Psalm 96:1-3)

There is something very special about daughters and dads.
And it's always a moment filled with all kinds of emotions when the daughter announces, "Dad, I want you to meet someone special."

Judy said, "I'm the oldest daughter and am now in college. When I told my dad I was bringing my first real boyfriend home to meet him, his response gave me cause for alarm. My dad said, 'I am going to be sitting on the front porch waiting with my shotgun!' I couldn't believe that he was saying it, but I was still going to bring Justin home to meet him.

"Then the day arrived and together we walked up to Dad's house. He wasn't on the porch. There was no shotgun. Justin was relieved. We walked in the house and there he sat watching television. I said, 'Hey, where's the shotgun?' He laughed and waved it off. He and Justin were a bit leery of each other but did the manly thing and shook hands. Soon, they were out on the porch talking. They have been talking ever since! In fact, they are such good friends I can hardly get in a word edgewise. It turned out just great!"

An introduction to any man that might take your daughter's heart away can be a threatening situation for a dad. Daddies want to be sure their girls end up with the best men possible! Not only is he being carefully scrutinized by his daughter for a reaction... he is risking a place forever in history in his daughter's eyes. It can be a very special "Hallmark" moment or it can be a disaster. It's a moment that dad and daughter can look back on and laugh. It's also a moment that causes many a husband to cringe when remembering.

What I Really Want

"Most importantly, I want to make sure that my daughter sees how much I love her mom and that I treat her mom with respect. Then she'll have a healthy concept when she's old enough to date. 'Cause if it's up to Daddy, she will never date. I want my child to grow up and be an independent and intelligent young woman, like her mother was when I married her. If she feels good about herself, she'll hopefully make the right decisions."

Dale, a dad on meeting a future son-in-law

Rejoice greatly, O daughter of Zion!
Shout, O daughter of Jerusalem!
Behold, your King is coming...
(Zechariah 9:9)

Much about the life of Charles de Gaulle, former prime minister of France, is quite well known and chronicled. What is not so widely known is Charles and Evonne de Gaulle were the parents of a "Down's syndrome" child. She was a treasure to them as well as a very special concern. Regardless of the affairs of state, de Gaulle arranged his life so he and his wife would have some time almost every day with their infant daughter. When they would put her to bed and the child had fallen asleep, Evonne would often ask, "Oh, Charles, why couldn't she have been like the others?"

As had been predicted by the attending physicians, de Gaulle's daughter died in her youth as a teen. There was a private, graveside Mass and when the priest had pronounced the benediction, all present began to leave… all, that is, except her mother.

In her grief, she could not seem to pull herself away. Charles went back to her, put an arm around her and very gently said, "Come, Evonne. Did you not hear the blessing of the priest? She is now like the others."

What a touchingly beautiful insight. Yes, people hurt and are in need of help in our world. Not everything is pleasant. Not everything works out like we think it should. There are parents who might also be standing beside the crib of their little one and wondering why or how such a thing is possible. One of the promises of the gospel of Jesus Christ is that a time is coming when the problems and limitations of this life will no longer govern our existence. A time is coming when all who are members of the kingdom of God will be set free from life's bondages! It's a day of promise!

Sing

Sing with all the sons and daughters of glory;
Sing the resurrection song!
Death and sorrow, earth's dark story,
To the former days belong!

William Irons

And I heard a loud voice from heaven saying,
"Behold, the tabernacle of God is with men, and He will dwell with
them, and they shall be His people.
God Himself will be with them and be their God.
And God will wipe away every tear from their eyes; there shall be no
more death, nor sorrow, nor crying.
There shall be no more pain, for the former things have passed away.
(Revelation 21:3-4)

A LITTLE CHILD SHALL LEAD THEM

It happened a number of years ago in my father's church when he was a pastor in Mansfield, Ohio. There was a family with an only child, a daughter. Mother and daughter were very faithful in church and Sunday school attendance. But the dad wasn't interested. It was okay for his wife and little girl to attend but not for him. He was quite a man… he worked in a steel mill, a hulk of a man who had played college football as an interior lineman. Tough and rough, good guy… but no time for church or God.

The daughter, Susie, became sick and was taken to the family doctor. The diagnosis was leukemia and because it had progressed to the final stages, there was nothing that could be done to save her. The family took her home to make her as comfortable as possible and care for her until death came.

Each night on coming home from work, the dad's first stop was Susie's bedroom-sickroom. He would visit with her and spend as much time with her as possible. Her condition worsened daily… she lost weight, her cheeks became sunken, her complexion grew pale.

One day in particular, Susie had obviously been doing some serious thinking, for she said to her dad, "Daddy, I know I will die soon and go to heaven to be with Jesus. My Sunday school teacher told me that when I get to heaven I will be given a crown to wear. But Daddy, my crown will have no stars because I have not helped anybody to know Jesus. So, Daddy, will you give your life to Jesus so I can have a star in my crown?"

This dad, through tears streaking down his cheeks, nodded his head and right then and there at her bedside prayed a sinner's prayer asking forgiveness and accepting

Jesus into his heart. It made Susie's eyes light up with joy. She called for her mother and told her what Daddy had just done. It was a glorious, happy time of hugging, crying and laughing together. About a week later Susie died.

On the Sunday morning following the funeral, Susie's dad went with her mother to church, for the first time. Time was taken in the service to allow time for a "testimony" and this dad stood and said: "I was resistant to the gospel and had rejected pastors and evangelists who had tried to lead me to Christ. I could easily reject all of these but I couldn't reject my little daughter." He paused to wipe away the tears and went on. "Because she loved me and asked me, I gave my life to Christ. She reached me when no one else could." Then, before he sat down, he looked upward and finished with this: "And now Susie is in heaven, wearing a crown promised to her and in it is a single star... that's me!"

Today's Quote

"Oh that someone would arise, man or God, to show us God!"

Socrates

Assuredly, I say to you, whoever does not receive the kingdom of God as a little child will by no means enter it.
(Mark 10:15)

GOAL SETTING

One of the most fascinating stories of goal setting comes out of the sports world. An eight-year-old boy told his dad and mother and everyone who would listen, "I'm going to be the greatest baseball catcher that ever lived!" Some people laughed at him. His mother patiently told him, "You are only eight years old; that's not the time to be talking about impossible dreams." He refused to listen to her or anybody else who attempted to talk him out of his goal. His dad said, "You can do it, but you must work very hard to reach it."

When he finished his high school career and walked across the platform in the gym to receive his diploma, he was stopped by the superintendent of schools who said, "Johnny, tell all these people what you want to be."

The young man squared his shoulders and said, "I am going to be the greatest baseball catcher that ever lived." Some snickered in the crowd. But that made no difference to Johnny.

Later, on one occasion, the then great manager of the New York Yankees, Casey Stengel, was asked about this young man. Casey replied like this: "Johnny Bench is already the greatest baseball catcher that has ever played the game!"

What makes this story so great? Already at age eight, Johnny Bench had set his goals. During his playing career he was twice voted MVP in major league baseball. It began with a dream, then became a goal which was lived out into reality!

Goals

Statistics tell me that if I were to poll the general population, less than 5% could tell me their life's goal!

Can we then conclude that 95 out of every 100 are simply moving with the tides of life?

Setting a goal for your life may well be one of the most important things you will ever do!

One More Thought

The Lord gave you two ends, one for sitting and one for thinking.

Your success depends on which you use...

Heads you win, tails you lose.

Do you not know that those who run in a race all run,
but one receives the prize?
Run in such a way that you may obtain it!
And everyone who competes for the prize is temperate in all things.
Now they do it to obtain a perishable crown, but we for an
imperishable crown.
(I Corinthians 9:24-25)

Dad, you may have all the "so-called skills" to be a father... but in becoming that father, please don't overlook this special ingredient. The following story says it better than I can...

A family back in the East, Pennsylvania to be exact, was planning a month's driving vacation to the West Coast. At the last minute the dad's work emergency prevented him from going... but Mom insisted that she was quite capable of following through with their plans and she and the kids would go ahead.

Dad got out the maps and planned the route of travel and where the family should be stopping at a motel each night. The plans were that dad should join them on the West Coast. But he finished his work earlier than planned and decided to surprise them. He booked his flight into a West Coast city without calling them. Then he took a taxi out into the country on a highway where, according to his travel plan, the family would be driving later in the day. The taxi driver dropped him off on the side of the road.

This dad waited patiently until he spotted the family car coming toward him and stuck out his thumb as a hitch-hiker. As Mom and the kids drove past, one of the kids shouted, "Hey, wasn't that Dad?"

Mom screeched to a stop, backed up to the hitch-hiker and the family had a joyful roadside reunion!

The cab driver called the newspaper and told them the story and a reporter tracked them down to their motel and interviewed the dad. He asked, "Why would you do such a crazy thing?"

Dad responded, "After I die, I want my kids to be able to say, 'Dad sure was fun, wasn't he?'"

Fathering

"The father is one of the most neglected figures of our time! His image has taken a plunge from the craggy dignity of Old Testament patriarchy; today if he is depicted in a television comedy he is usually shown as a buffoon. The father for the moment is an endangered species... to be preserved, if at all, only by careful thought and planning."

Maureen Green

As for Me, behold, My covenant is with you, and you shall be a father of many...
(Genesis 17:4)

DAD ALWAYS SAID

- By the time you get to the point where you can make ends meet... somebody moves the ends.
- You are not a carpenter until you've run one finger through the saw; if you run too many fingers through the saw, you're not a carpenter.
- Anything that begins well ends badly. Anything that begins badly ends up worse.
- Work is the crab grass of life, but money is the water that keeps it green.
- Money is the root of all evil and man needs roots. But it's not really the money... it's the principal and interest of the thing.
- When you find something you like, stock up... they're going to quit making it.
- Almost everything in life is easier to get into than to get out of.
- When you are right, no one remembers. When you are wrong, no one ever forgets.
- The less influence or money you have, the longer you will wait.
- Anticipate trouble... but don't go looking for it.
- Every man has a scheme that won't work.
- Either the box is too small and won't work, or it's too big and won't fit... when all else fails, read the instructions.
- The best dressed army always loses.
- Ask your mother.

THE 'DAD' FACTOR

You're watching the NBA finals or the NFL championship or the NCAA finals. It's a time out and a bench cam focuses on a player, he grins, he raises his index finger upward, looks into the lens and says, "Hi, Dad!" Sure... and Dick Vitale is a monk!

As any sports fan knows, the on-camera anthem of athletes is not sung to Dad...but it goes like this, "Hi, Mom!" Yet there are a number of players who know mom needs some help and they are not afraid to express it.

Think with me about the "dad-advantage" some players have... athletes who are respectable role models, who love God and who give credit to their Dad.

One is Charlie Ward, the Heisman Trophy winning former quarterback of the Florida State Seminoles. Charlie Sr. was involved in Junior's life. When in high school, his dad was his assistant football and basketball coach. Charlie credits his parents... both of them... with being "the main leaders in my life."

Former NBA player, A. C. Green, who was named after his father, also credits his father A. C. Sr. with setting the tone for his life. "My father was a great example. He taught me to work hard, to have a strong work ethic. He would work two or three jobs, if necessary, to provide for his family."

Avery Johnson, quick little point guard of Golden State, minces no words in talking about his dad. A. J. says, "He taught me how to be a man... a godly man. He taught me how to be a father and how to provide for my family. My father and I had a great relationship."

David Robinson is grateful to his dad, Ambrose, a Navy man about whom David says, "He was the biggest influence on my life."

A New Trend?

"Perhaps dads Ward, Green, Johnson, Robinson, are on the cutting edge of a new trend, one in which dads from all socioeconomic strata recognize the positive impact they can have. The more dads do that, the easier life will be for everybody, Mom included."

Dave Branon, Sports Spectrum

When you eat the labor of your hands,
You shall be happy, and it shall be well with you.
Your wife shall be like a fruitful vine
In the very heart of your house.
Your children like olive plants all around your table.
Behold, thus shall the man be blessed
Who fears the Lord.
(Psalm 128:2-4)

I HAVE ASKED TOO MUCH

Listen, son, I am saying this as you lie asleep, one little paw crumpled under your cheek and the blond curls stuck to your damp forehead. I have crept into your room alone. Just a few minutes ago, as I sat reading my paper, a stifling wave of remorse swept over me. Guilty, I came to your bedside.

These are things I was thinking, son: I had been cross to you. I scolded you as you dressed for school because you only gave your face a dab with a towel. I took you to task for not cleaning your shoes. I called out in anger when you threw some of your things on the floor.

At breakfast, I found fault, too. You spilled things. You ate with your hands. You gulped down your food. You put your elbows on the table. You spread butter too thick on your toast. And as you started off to school and I made for my ride, you turned and waved and called out, "Goodbye, Daddy!" and I frowned and said in reply, "Hold your shoulders back!"

Then it began all over again in the late afternoon. As I came up the road I spied you, down on your knees playing. There were holes in your jeans. I humiliated you before your friends by marching you ahead of me to the house. Jeans are expensive and if you had to buy them you would learn to be more careful! Imagine that, son, from your dad!

Do you remember, later, when I was reading my paper on the sofa, how you came over, timidly, with a sort of hurt look in your eyes? When I glanced up over my paper, impatient at the interruption, you hesitated. "What is it you want?" I snapped.

You said nothing but ran across the room in one tempestuous plunge and threw your arms around my neck and kissed me, your small arms tightened with an affection that God had set blooming in your heart and which even neglect and criticism could not wither. And then you were gone, pattering up the stairs to your bedroom.

Well, son, it was shortly afterward that my paper slipped from my hands and a terrible sickening fear came over me. What has habit been doing to me? The habit of finding fault, of reprimanding... this was my reward to you for being a boy. It was not that I did not love you; it was that I expected too much of you. It was measuring you by the yardstick of my own years.

And there was so much that was good and fine and true in your character. That little heart of yours was as big as the dawn itself over the wide hills. This was shown by your spontaneous impulse to rush in and kiss me good-night. Nothing else matters tonight, son. I have come to your bedside in the darkness and I have knelt here, ashamed!

It is a feeble atonement. I know you would not understand these things if I told them to you during your waking hours. But tomorrow I will be a real daddy! I will chum with you and suffer when you suffer and laugh when you laugh. I will bite my tongue when impatient words come. I will keep saying as if it were a ritual: "He is nothing but a boy... a little boy!"

I am afraid I have visualized you as a man. Yet as I see you now, son, crumpled, and weary on your bed, I see that you are still a baby. Yesterday you were in your mother's arms, your head on her shoulder. I have asked too much, too much.

W. Livingston Larned, Westminster Bible Class, adapted   & condensed

A 'D' IN CALCULUS

My dad found me crying in my bedroom after the first day of class, my senior year in high school. I hated school, but I knew that I had to go to repeat junior calculus. From grade school, I'd been in the mentally gifted program and was used to getting As and Bs in my classes. But during my junior year, I took an advanced calculus class in which the teacher decided to grade on the curve. This meant that some of us would have to fail.

The end of my junior year, my report card had a D next to calculus, a grade I had never had before. My parents were very upset and my father told me that I'd have to take the class over and raise my grade. All summer long I dreaded returning to school. When the day came, all I could do was cry.

When my dad found out why I was sobbing, he said something remarkable to me. He said, "You are more important to me than a grade. You have outgrown high school and need new experiences, so forget repeating calculus. For me to make you do that would simply be a matter of pride. I'll do what I can to help you graduate early." If I'd ever doubted it before, I knew for sure that day that my dad had his own way of living life, full of grace. He believed there were many ways of getting to a goal, and saw possibilities where others might have seen only one way. He passed it on to me.

I can think of no more rewarding task than to tell the world I love my daddy. Not only that, I respect and admire him. This… is a tribute to a dad named David Berry, who loved his daughter well, and who will never be forgotten.

Carmen Renee Berry, co-author, Daddies and Daughters,
Simon & Schuster, 1998, adapted, condensed

More Feeling

"Arthur always has his arms around (his daughter) Camera.
When he talked about her, his face would light up like
stars in the sky.
He showed more feeling for his daughter than I had seen him
show his whole life."

Harace Ashe, uncle of Arthur Ashe

Behold, children are a heritage from the Lord,
The fruit of the womb is a reward.
Like arrows in the hand of a warrior,
So are the children of one's youth.
Happy is the man who has his quiver full of them;
They shall not be ashamed.
(Psalm 127:3-5)

THE BLACK DOOR

Several generations ago, during one of the most turbulent desert wars in the Middle East, a spy was captured. The general of the Persian army, a man of intelligence and compassion, had adopted an unusual custom in such cases. He permitted the prisoner to make a choice of either facing the execution squad or passing through the black door.

As the moment of execution drew near, the general ordered the spy to be brought before him for the final interview. "What shall it be, the execution squad or the black door?"

The convicted spy hesitated. Finally he chose the execution squad. Not long after, noise of the execution in the courtyard announced the grim sentence had been carried out. The general stared at his boots. Then he turned to his aide and said, "You see how it is with men? They will always prefer the known to the unknown, even if it means facing certain death. It is characteristic of people to be afraid of the undefined."

"What lies beyond the black door?" asked the aide.

"Freedom," replied the general, "and I've known only a few men brave enough to take it."

We face the unknown in everyday life. Our choices won't always be a matter of life or death… but taking risks with the unknown may increase our freedom and success. We tend to get into the rut of life and settle for mediocrity. Failure has humbled and dulled us to the point that we can't recognize our own potential. We lack the guts to stop living our lives in a mentally-chloroformed condition of non-commitment!

The Next Time...
You are faced with a choice, remember the story of the spy, the general, the black door and freedom!

Today's Quote
"The one thing that will guarantee the successful conclusion of a doubtful undertaking is faith in the beginning that you can do it!"
William James

Then Caleb quieted the people before Moses, and said,
"Let us go up at once and take possession,
for we are well able to overcome it.
(Numbers 13:30)

The blue-tick hound had bayed the sun into orbit, now he is running low-bellied with nose pressed to the trail. The strong scent of bear intoxicated his brain and the splay-footed tracks drew him magnetically on.

Suddenly... the warmer trail of a deer crossed his path, it must be much closer. He swung to follow it, halfway down the hollow the hot spoor of a rabbit tied his hungry stomach in knots. The blue tick turned in full voice to trail the rabbit.

He soon lost the track and the rabbit when he paused to trace the tantalizing scent of a chipmunk which ended in a rock pile. At evening time, his master found him... excitedly circling a tall reed, at the top of which cowered a little field mouse.

A simple parable of a loose-brained, undisciplined hound dog. Yes and more. It's the story of too many men who started out in life after great quarry, intoxicated with dreams of certain success but ended life's chase with nothing more than a mouse.

Many a man has begun life with flawless ideals and far-reaching plans but somehow they have been discarded in the heat of the race. At the end of the day when the Master asks for an accounting, he has nothing to show for it but a trifle or two. But that's not the way life should be lived!

To be a man... you must be discerning! You have to choose and choose rightly. Choose now or you will dash through life switching from one track to another, never knowing, never discovering what life can be at its best. Look around you... it holds possibilities you've hardly dreamed of!

Discerning...

Life is so short and of such great importance... time is so perishable and so priceless, there is no time for toying with the bad or dabbling with the doubtful or going after the good!
The good isn't good enough!
You don't even have time for the urgent...
You have time only for the best! The very best!!

"Resolved, to live every moment of my life with all of my ability, and to make every decision so that I will have no regrets one hundred years hence!"

Jonathan Edwards

I can do all things through Christ who strengthens me!
(Philippians 4:13)

TO BE A MAN...BE BELIEVABLE

I looked at the letter, it was marked, "THIS IS A PERSONAL LETTER FROM GOD!" I couldn't believe my eyes... I read it again. Sure enough, that's exactly what it said and a whole lot more. The post mark? A Midwestern city in the U.S.A. I hadn't known that God now lived in Missouri with His own address.

A personal letter from God... now that was really something! I've always wanted to get one of those. But there were some hitches as I began reading with a curious mind. Why couldn't He spell my name correctly? Why was the print-out so poor? Sure enough... it was as phony as a $3 bill! I didn't even bother to finish reading it. It was placed in file #13... the round one that gets emptied just about every day.

Everything a man reads, hears or sees must pass the test of believability! Especially in America! When Princess Margaret of Great Britain was to travel to America for the first time, British journalist, Alan Whicker, gave her this advice: "When you travel to America allow 10% for oversell." I don't know if that's enough. Then there was another Englishman who said: "Believe only half of what you see and nothing of what you hear."

Things are so wildly oversold that even the most gullible among us thinks twice before buying or believing... especially during the political races. Your fellow men are constantly shifting smooth sales pitches, ads, blurbs, speeches, gimmicks and commercials. And they apply the same test to you and your life: IS IT BELIEVABLE? IS HE BELIEVABLE?

Today's Thought

Reputation is what you are said to be... character is what you are.
Reputation is a picture... character is your real face.
Reputation is what you have when you move into a new
community or new job... character is what you have
when you leave.
Reputation goes and can grow like a mushroom...
character is built in a lifetime.
Reputation is what will be said at your funeral... character is what
you will or won't be before the Judge of all mankind.

*What's the use of saying that you have faith and are Christians
if you aren't proving it by helping others?
Will that kind of faith save anyone?
Faith without good deeds is dead and useless... faith that does
not result in good deeds is not real faith.
(James 2:14, 17, 20, Living Letters)*

LOSER'S LIMP

"Watch this," chuckled the coach, as together we watched his team compete in a track meet. "You see my boy there, coming in fourth. Limping! He was favored to win this 200. Chances are he just developed that limp to have an excuse for not doing better. I call it loser's limp."

Sure enough... he limped over to the coach's side and said, "Coach, I just couldn't do it, something happened in my leg." The coach looked over at me and winked.

I've thought about that a number of times since... Some of the reasons why men don't reach their goals are no more convincing than the high school boy's suddenly developed limp as an excuse. Worse yet, the loser's limp attitude can stop a man from even trying to lift his life to the next level. When the gun goes off to start the race, with his loser's limp excuse, he is licked before the race begins.

Now this man can be very convincing, "You can see how badly I was outnumbered... the odds were against me." Or "I was working in a no-win situation..." Or... or... or... Rarely is it a real handicap.

Now, I'm not talking about people who are blind, although you can learn a life lesson from Helen Keller. I'm not talking about wheel-chair bound men such as James Royce, immobilized by polio, who built a thriving business from his bed and chair. Hats off to these who overcome.

I'm talking about men who have adopted a built-in loser's limp as life's excuse when they come up short. I'm talking to you, DAD, if you have never taken charge of your life-dynamics because of a loser's limp!

Today's Quote

"Sir... if you've lost a few of life's races, see if you're not assum-
ing you're a loser forever,
If you're not acquiring a loser's limp before you start."

J. K. Summerhill

> *But Jesus looked at them and said,*
> *"With men it is impossible, but not with God;*
> *FOR WITH GOD ALL THINGS ARE POSSIBLE!"*
> *(Mark 10:27)*

I KNEW I COULD

Mike Craig was the heavy weight wrestler on the Central High School, St. Joseph, Missouri, team during the years my sons, Marc and Kirk, were also varsity wrestlers. Mike was a good kid in spite of a difficult home situation and a very determined, committed kid. He was the largest boy to try out for the team, but still a very light heavy weight… but he was the only one available. His first year, Mike lost every single match. It was painful to watch.

The second year he won a very few… his junior year he won more and managed to win through regionals to go to state. He lost his first and second match and was eliminated.

But in his senior year… things were different. Mike was seasoned and had a great attitude. He won every match! He competed at state and there he won everything. Now he was ready for the championship match. I remind you, Mike weighed a light 205 pounds… his opponent from St. Louis had never lost a match in his career and weighed in at 352 pounds! Talk about David against Goliath.

The first period… no points were scored. Second period, Mike began in the "down" position… he managed an escape scoring one point. Third period begins, his opponent is in the down position and escaped scoring one point. The match is tied, one to one with seconds left. The crowd is on its feet screaming… this is the last match of the state tournament. Mike had been carefully working him, round and round, careful not to get caught. The coach had told Mike to work him, tire him out, set him up for Mike's favorite take-down move. With less than six seconds left, Mike like a cat, reached in and took him down with an "ankle pick" scoring two points… and put him on his back scoring three more! Mike Craig was state heavyweight champion in the large school class with a six to one score!

I asked Mike, after the match, "How did you do it?"

He smiled and said, "Mr. Strand, I had faith in myself. I knew I could beat him if I was patient and set him up. AND... I didn't give up!"

Today's Thought

Why should we have to "contend" for anything in life?
Everything in life is attained through an effort including spiritual goals, mental goals, financial goals, family goals and a successful lifestyle.
To contend for anything implies a fight...two parties contending for the prize.
If we do not fight for the faith, our faith, we lose it.

*For we do not wrestle against flesh and blood, but against principalities, against powers, against the rulers of the darkness of this age, against spiritual hosts of wickedness in the heavenly places.
Therefore take up the whole armor of God,
That you may be able to withstand in the evil day, and having done all, to stand! (Ephesians 6:12-13)*

THAT CONSTANT PRACTICE

At the major university in Hiedelburg, Germany, in the music department, there was a piano instructor who was simply and affectionately known as "Pops" or just "Herman." He was like a father to all his students. One night at a special university sponsored concert, with a standing-room-only crowd, a world-renown concert pianist suddenly became sick while performing an extremely difficult piece and had to leave the stage.

No sooner had the artist rushed off the stage than "Pops Herman" rose from his seat in the audience, walked on stage, sat down at the piano and with great mastery finished the piece beginning with the exact notes where the guest had stopped! Not only did he finish this piece... he completed the entire repertoire in place of the stricken guest pianist. When completed there was a thunderous, standing ovation which went on and on in his honor.

Later that evening, at a party, one of the students asked Herman how he was able to complete and perform such a demanding concert so beautifully and without a rehearsal.

Herman replied, "In 1939, when I was a budding young concert pianist, I was arrested and placed in a Nazi concentration camp. Putting it mildly, the future looked bleak. But I knew that in order to keep the flicker of hope and faith alive that I might someday play again... I needed to practice every day. I began by fingering a piece from my repertoire on my bare-board bed late one night. The next night I added a second piece and soon I was running through a whole list of music. I did this every night for five long years. It so happens that the pieces I played tonight at the concert hall were all a part of that repertoire."

He looked affectionately at the questioning student and concluded, "That constant practice is what kept my hopes and faith alive. Everyday, I renewed my hope and faith that I would one day be able to play my music again… on a real piano… and in freedom!"

Today's Thought
That's it… take the faith God has given you, practice with it on a daily basis and don't give up on it in spite of what might happen to you!

For by grace you have been saved through faith, and that not of
yourselves; it is the gift of God,
not of works, lest anyone should boast.
For we are His workmanship, created in Christ Jesus for good
works, which God prepared beforehand that we
should walk in them.
(Ephesians 2:8-10)

QUOTABLE QUOTES FROM DADS

My father used to play with my brother and me in the yard. Mother would come out and say, "You're tearing up the grass."

"We're not raising grass," Dad would reply, "We're raising boys."
(Harmon Killebrew, baseball Hall of Famer)

My father didn't tell me how to live; he lived, and let me watch him do it.
(Clarence Budington Kelland)

Find a copy of Martin Luther King's "I Have a Dream" speech and read it aloud to your children. Encourage them to revel in the virtues of America that the late preacher so eloquently extolled.
(Chris Rodell)

Human beings are the only creatures on earth that allow their children to come back home.
(Bill Cosby)

Children brighten up a household. They never turn the lights off.
(Ralph Bus)

It is much easier to become a father than to be one.
(Ken Nerburn)

The license plate on a sporty red BMW convertible seen on Florida roads could explain why the guy driving was smiling: "KIDSGON"
(Unknown)

One father is worth more than a hundred schoolmasters.
(George Herbert)

Grandchildren are God's reward for not killing your own children.
(Unknown Dad)

You don't really understand human nature unless you know why a child on a merry-go-round will wave at his parents every time around... and why his parents will always wave back.
(William d. Tammeus)

Children are a great comfort in your old age... and they help you reach it faster, too!
(Lionel Kauffman)

Always kiss your children goodnight... even when they're asleep.
(H. Jackson Brown, Jr.)

All those years I was a young actor in Hollywood, I never dreamed my son would wind up owning it.
(Kirk Douglas on son, Michael)

It costs approximately $160,000 to raise a child until he or she is fifteen. That's about $8,889 a year, or $741 a month, or $171 a week, or $24 a day, or $1 an hour. Not a bad deal, considering you get naming rights.
(Chris Rodell)

Parents often talk about the younger generation as if they've had nothing to do with it.
(Haim Ginott)

Don't worry that children never listen to you; worry that they are always watching you.
(Robert Fulghum)

There are two lasting bequests we can give our children. One is roots. The other is wings.
(Hodding Carter)

Each day of our lives we make deposits in the memory banks of our children.
(Charles Swindoll)

"Don't Feed the Seagulls" is a book dedicated to my father. Dr. Dale Ursini von Rosenberg was an exceptionally intelligent man who saw the beauty and nature of God in many things: the laws of mathematics that he knew and loved so well, baseball, music, a good book, God's great out-of-doors and especially friends and family. He gave expression to his knowledge through the love he poured out to those around him. And he was greatly blessed to spend the last 49 years of his life as Marjorie's husband.

My father battled ALS the last two and half years of his life. He fought valiantly and used all his strength, his will and his faith to sustain himself. As he counted the days, hours and minutes until everyone arrived, he seemed like the marathon runner entering the stadium for the final lap. With no energy left, he looked within and found a deep resolve; he looked about and found the support of his family and friends and he looked above and found the greatest strength of all. Then, like that tired marathon runner, he willed himself forward, across the finish line. We lifted him on our shoulders for a victory lap and then God lifted him higher to glory in heaven.

I watched my father's struggle and asked God to help me understand. The following is a prayer and conversation between God, a father and a son.

LOOK AT MY HANDS

Look at my hands, now crippled and old,
Once so strong, now what can they hold?
THEY HOLD THE LOVE I GAVE TO YOU,
YOU PASSED IT ON, YET IT STAYED AND GREW.
I felt it Dad, when you held me high,
I laughed and sang and touched the sky.
I felt God's love when you passed it through
And now I'm here to bring it back to you.

Look at my feet, I can barely stand,
They climbed tall mountains and crossed the land!
THEY CARRY THE MESSAGE OF JESUS' LOVE
HIGHER THAN MOUNTAINTOPS TO HEAVEN ABOVE.
I followed you Dad, to that highest peak
And I followed you Dad, our Savior to seek.
Your feet led me to Him when I was a boy
With Him in our hearts, each day filled with joy.

It's so hard to breathe, the air is so thin,
I want to shout and sing praises again.
I STILL HEAR THE SONGS AND THE PRAISES YOU LIFT,
COME SING THEM IN HEAVEN WHERE NEW LIFE IS YOUR GIFT!
You taught me to sing Dad, with you I give praise
And I thank God today I was your son to raise.
All of your family and your many friends too,
Each of us, all of us, see Jesus in you.

He's my Daddy, Lord, I can't say good-bye,
Whatever you do, please don't let him die!
THE LOVE THAT I GAVE HIM HE PASSED ON TO YOU,
NOW PASS IT TO OTHERS AND WATCH IT RENEW.
Don't fret over me, son, I've been born again,
I'm living in heaven and free from all sin.
My hands are strong, my feet can run,
Hear me shout, "Hallelujah, the victory's won!"

*Dedicated to Dr. Dale U. von Rosenberg, written by his
son, Byron von Rosenberg, June 24, 2002, taken from
Don't Feed the Seagulls (ACW Press 2003)*

THE MASTER OF SACK

Peter Boulware is a scary guy, especially if you are playing football and most scary of all if you happen to be the opposing team's quarterback! He's 6-foot-4-inches, 255 pounds and runs the 40-yard dash in 4.54 seconds. Not only that, he has a 37 inch vertical leap and bench-presses more than 400 pounds! He's the outside linebacker for the Baltimore Ravens professional football team.

His awards range from a first team All-American his junior year, a first-round pick in the NFL draft, defensive rookie of the year (1997), three appearances in the Pro Bowl and a Super Bowl ring (2000) along with other accolades too numerous to list here. He is considered to be the prototypical linebacker with an insatiable desire to wreak havoc on an opponent's offense and he becomes a one-man wrecking crew, on the football field.

But off the field... you see something different. As he gives an interview to reporters, he's humble, sincere and enthusiastic. He's one of the team, one of the guys. Is there a secret to this man? Boulware is quick to tell you that football playing is more than a job... it's a ministry!

"I play well so I can represent God," he says. "Through Him elevating me and giving me a platform, I can share what He has done for me." It almost sounds too good to be true. But press him a bit more and his response is, "I play to glorify the Lord. Win or lose, good or bad, I am going to play as hard as I can so that I glorify Him."

One of the disciplines in his life to help him keep strong in the faith is depending on other Christians to pray for him and hold him accountable. "On my own I can't do it, having strong Christians around me keeping me accountable and standing with me when times get hard... that's the only way I am making it because every day it's a battle."

JOHN WOODEN

There's never been a finer man in American sports than John Wooden! He won ten NCAA basketball championships at UCLA, the last was in 1975. Nobody has come within six of his record.

He won 88 straight games between January 30, 1971 and January 17, 1974. Nobody has come within 42 since.

There has never been another coach like Wooden, quiet as an April snow and square as a game of checkers; loyal to one woman (53 years), one school, one way... walking about the campus in his sensible shoes and Jimmy Stewart morals.

He'd spend a half hour the first day of practice teaching his men how to put on a sock. "Wrinkles can lead to blisters," he'd warn. These players would sneak looks at each other and roll their eyes. Eventually they'd do it right. "Good," he'd say, "and now for the other foot."

Of the 180 players who played for him, Wooden knows the whereabouts of 172. Of course, it's not hard when most of them call, checking on his health, secretly hoping to hear some of his simple life lessons so they can write them on the lunch bags of their kids, who will roll their eyes.

"Discipline yourself, and others won't need to," Coach would say. "Never lie, never cheat, never steal," and "Earn the right to be proud and confident."

If you played for him, you played by his rules: Never score without acknowledging a teammate. One word of profanity and you're done for the day. Treat your opponent with respect.

No UCLA basketball jersey number was retired under his watch. "What about the fellows who wore that number before? Didn't they contribute to the team?" he'd say.

He believed in hopelessly out-of-date stuff that never did anything but win championships. No dribbling behind the back or through the legs. "There's no need," he'd say.

No long hair, no facial hair. "They take too long to dry and you could catch cold leaving the gym," he'd say. That one drove his players bonkers.

One day, All-American center Bill Walton showed up with a full beard. "It's my right," he insisted. Wooden asked if he believed that strongly. Walton said he did. "That's good, Bill," Coach said. "I admire people who have strong beliefs and stick by them, I really do. We're going to miss you." Walton shaved it right then and there. Now Walton calls once a week to tell Coach he loves him.

It's almost as though we have been visiting him at his modest condo and it's too soon to go back into a world where the rules are now much grayer and the teams so much worse.

As Wooden ushers us to the door... we take one last look around. The framed report cards of his great-grandkids, the boxes of jelly beans peeking out from under the favorite chair and the dozens of pictures of Nellie.

He's ninety now. A little more hunched over than the last time we stopped by. Steps are a little smaller. We hope it's not the last time we see him or hear from him. He smiles, "I'm not afraid to die," he says. "Death is my only chance to be with her again."

The problem is, we still need him and his influence here.

A MOUNTAIN-CLIMBING MILLIONAIRE

Not yet thirty, Billie is a self-made millionaire! He doesn't drink, smoke or dance and he gives lavish sums to politicians. Everyone, it seems, wants Billie's opinion. Even the President of the United States solicited Billie's advice. Billie is on top of the world. He's made it to the peak of the mountain. It just doesn't get any better than this.

As he accepted his award from the Junior Chamber of Commerce as one of America's outstanding young men, Billie said, "I owe my success to clean living." When these awards were over, Billie chuckles to a friend, "They'll never catch up with me. These people are stupid."

With his warm handshake and winning smile, Billie romanced wealthy private investors and secured massive government funding for more than 33,000 rural fertilizer storage tanks. He then purchased a few hundred tanks and scattered them across West Texas. Tens of millions of dollars go into Billie's pocket.

A friend asked Billie where he got the inspiration for his scheme and he explained how Texas ranchers have borrowed heavily from a bank, using their cattle for collateral and have then driven bankers around on huge tracks of land to get a general count of cattle. "Those bankers never realize they're counting the same cows over and over from different vantage points on the ranch," so said Billie. "It'll be the same way with my storage tanks. I'll starve them to death looking for my equipment."

When he was young, Billie Sol Estes had a plan for getting rich quick and it worked. He made it to the top of the mountain. Now in his seventies, Billie has spent most of his adult life in prison because he was a brilliant schemer who told himself, "Time is the enemy. Hard work is for others. Cleverness is the key to success."

Today's Quotes

"There is no royal road to anything.
One thing at a time, and all things in succession.
That which grows slowly endures."

Josiah G. Holland

Time is your ally. Hard work is inevitable. Persistence is the key to lasting success. The best way to climb a mountain is to take one small step after another!

Today's Questions

Which of these ideologies best describes your belief system?
Do you consider time your enemy or friend?
Is hard work a thing to be escaped or embraced?
Do you depend more on your cleverness or your persistence?

*"If the ax is dull, And one does not sharpen the edge,
Then he must use more strength; But wisdom brings success!"
(Ecclesiastes 10:10)*

TALK ABOUT BAD LUCK

Dean Rhoads met Dave Thomas long before Dave opened his first Wendy's. "Fort Wayne wasn't a large town in those days, so when I needed an extra hand, I'd often call on young Dave to help me out. It's a great pity for me that I didn't invest in Wendy's," says Dean, "because I really liked the boy and I always knew that he would someday do something big."

Strike one!

Dave then worked at the local Kentucky Fried Chicken location, one of the Colonel's first. Through Dave "I met Colonel Sanders," says Dean, "and I had opportunity to buy stock in his company early on, but I didn't agree with some of his ideas, so I didn't invest in it."

Strike two!

Dean, like Thomas and Sanders, was also a pioneer in food service. It was his company that perfected the first system for keeping food hot while waiting to be served. Despite every effort... it didn't succeed.

Rhoads continues, "One of the salesman attempting to sell me something was named Ray. He sold a gadget called a multi-mixer that mixed five milk shakes at the same time. I heard that Ray Kroc had bought a little hamburger stand called McDonalds, I chose not to invest."

Strike three!

While on a cruise I met an attorney from the Pacific Northwest who told funny stories about how his son Billy and friends would sit at the kitchen table and attempt to make useful gadgets from baskets of electronic components. He told me his son was really bright and that I should invest in his new company, "Microsoft!"

What's soft about an electronic gadget? So I didn't invest.

Strike four!

How about that? Isn't the batter supposed to leave the batter's box after the third strike? You might think that all Dean Rhoads does is tell these sad stories. Not so. He did not give up. Dean pursued his own dream and invested in himself until the day came when his name reached #289 on the Forbes list of the 400 most successful business owners in America. The little company, Lincoln Manufacturing, that couldn't meet the payroll has an annual volume approaching $700 million!

Today's Quote

"In this game of life, there is no rule that says you have to leave the batter's box after your third strike!

If you're smart, you'll do just like Dean Rhoads and keep on swinging until you finally hit the home run!

The game's not over until you walk away from the plate!"

Roy H. Williams

And not only that, but we also glory in tribulations, knowing that tribulation produces perseverance; and perseverance, character; and character, hope!

(Romans 5:3, 4)

ARE YOU BEHIND OR LEADING?

Louis L'Amour, the prolific writer of novels about our American West, wrote a short story describing a man who loved books:

The man was noticed acting suspiciously as he perused the shelves in a public library. He took down a leather-bound copy of Shakespeare's *King Lear* and ran his fingers gently over the cover. He opened the book and felt the pages. Suddenly he tucked it under his coat and bolted out the door.

Someone who had been watching him ran after the thief and stopped him. The man willingly surrendered the book. Then he explained. All his life he had loved books, but he had never learned to read. So he would come to the library just to hold books. He loved the way they felt in his hands. That's why he had stolen Shakespeare.

Think of the people… fathers included, who can read but have no passion for learning or reading. Their crime equals or is greater than L'Amour's character. Mark Twain said, "The man who does not read good books has no advantage over the man who can't read them."

Victor Hugo put it like this: "It is those books which a man possesses but does not read which constitute the most significant evidence against him."

Motivational speaker Jim Rohn advocates that to become a high achiever we must read. He suggests disciplining ourselves to read two books per week. That's about 100 books a year. He quips: "If you've done that for the last 10 years, you're 1,000 books ahead. If you haven't, you're 1,000 books behind!"

Dad… one of the greatest gifts you can give to your children is the love of reading. Read books to them and with them. I know that generally men are not the readers that ladies are. In fact, women purchase and read more than 70% of all the books sold.

Today's Quote

"Just the knowledge that a good book is awaiting one at the end of a long day makes that day happier!"

Kathleen Norris

If the above is true... you're probably ahead.
If not, you're getting more behind every day!

Ten years from now... you will have been changed for the better because of the people you meet and the books you read!
PEOPLE YOU MEET AND THE BOOKS YOU READ!

"Your Word I have hidden in my heart,
That I might not sin against YOU!"
(Psalm 119:11)

Coach Bill McCartney tells about the time in 1991, while coaching football at the University of Colorado, that he challenged his team to play beyond their normal abilities. He had heard that we spend 86% of our time thinking about ourselves and 14% of our time thinking of others. The coach was convinced that if his team could stop thinking about themselves and begin to think of others, there would be a whole new source of energy.

He challenged each of the team members to call someone he admired and loved and tell the person that he was dedicating the next game to them. The team member was to encourage this person to carefully watch every play he made, because it was all dedicated and played for this special person. McCartney planned to distribute sixty footballs, one for each player to send to the person he had chosen with the final score written on the football.

The team Colorado was playing was arch-rival Nebraska Cornhuskers on their home turf in Lincoln. Colorado had not won a game there in 23 years! But Coach had just challenged his players to play beyond themselves, to play for the love of the game, to play for the love of another person.

The Colorado Buffaloes won the football game! The final score, along with an autograph from the individual player, was written on sixty different footballs. The final score? 27 to 12!

Do you think this ploy of thinking of another person made that big of a difference? Was this sufficient motivation to allow the Buffaloes to win the 24th game in this series?

Adapted from What Makes a Man? 12 Promises That Will Change Your Life
by Bill McCartney, NavPress, pp. 12-13

Imposed or Exposed Leadership?

"Jesus' authority was not something imposed on others, but rather a force He exposed!

His authority was the exposing of an inner spiritual power that was released little by little... through words, actions, attitudes, and His very presence... until finally His character itself seemed to be as wonderful as His greatest miracle."

Leighton Ford

Let this mind be in you which was also in Christ Jesus!
(Philippians 2:5)

THE VOICE FROM ABOVE

It seems these two big city coaches from the Miami professional hockey team were scouting through the state of Minnesota to find future players. While on this particular scouting trip during winter, they heard about one of the specialties of the area... ice fishing. So they decided to attempt it. They went to a sporting goods store and asked how they should go about ice fishing. They were told how to do it and what they would need to be ice fishermen. They bought all the required paraphernalia... lines, poles, artificial lures, bait, power saw, a tent, a Coleman stove, power drill, boots, parkas, fishing license... the whole bit, etc. Then they found a patch of ice, pitched their tent and began cutting a hole in the ice.

Just as they were getting into the spirit of the thing, a loud awesome voice from above proclaimed: "There are no fish under the ice!" That stopped them for a moment but they looked quizzically at each other, too embarrassed to acknowledge this eerie voice. They turned back to the drill and the ice. Just as they got going again they heard the voice repeat: "There are no fish under the ice!" They stole embarrassed looks at each other but kept drilling.

Now... a third time, even louder than before the booming voice thundered at them: "THERE ARE NO FISH UNDER THE ICE!"

Finally, one of them could not stand it any longer so he stood up and shouted, "Is that you, Lord?"

Again, the voice boomed back: "NO, this is the manager of the ice skating rink!"

Today's Thought

An optimist is a person who saves the pictures in the seed catalog to compare them with the flowers and veggies he grows. A pessimist is the optimist at harvest time.

> *To everything there is a season,*
> *A time for every purpose under heaven:*
> *A time to laugh;*
> *A time to mourn.*
> *(Ecclesiastes 3:1, 4)*

DAD'S CHOICE

My son's birthday was a few weeks away and I hadn't given much thought to a gift. He would be eight and he changed his mind about almost everything every day… the food he liked, favorite pajamas, games and especially toys or books. I listened and kept my ears open for a clue.

I overheard him tell his older brother that he wanted a soccer ball for his birthday. "Great," I thought, "that settles that. Now I can get back to other things." Of course my wife, Liz, had a few things picked out for him. But I wanted something appropriate for a "manly" dad to give a son. No socks or underwear for me. A few days later, the two boys and I were watching a football game. During a time-out he said, "Can I have a new football for my birthday?" I was confused. Football or soccer ball?

Time slipped by. Then just two days before his birthday, I decided he was old enough to have a serious talk with dad about giving gifts. In my study, we closed the door, and I said, "Steven, you are going to be eight years old Saturday. You are growing up to be a fine young man. I want to get you something nice and I'd like to surprise you. But I had rather get you something you really want. What do you want for your birthday? I've heard you mention a football or a soccer ball and I'd like to get you both, and someday I will, but which would you really rather have now? Football or soccer ball?"

He didn't hesitate. "I'd really rather have a football but if every time I ask you to play catch with me, you're going to tell me you're too busy, then just get me a soccer ball, cause I can always play with that by myself."

I sat there is stunned silence. "Okay," I finally said. The next morning I headed for "Four Star Sports" and bought a genuine, regulation, leather NFL licensed football. As I carried it to the car, I silently prayed, "Lord, please help me to give time to my son just as I give him this ball. And…Lord, thank you that you are never too busy to spend time with me!"

Jon H. Allan

A PRAYER ON BEING A FATHER

Dear Heavenly Father:

Make me a better father. Help me to understand my children, to listen patiently to what they have to say and to answer all their questions kindly. Keep me from interrupting them, talking back to them and contradicting them. Make me as courteous to them as I would have them be to me. Give me the courage to confess my sins against my children and ask them forgiveness, when I know I have done wrong.

Forbid that I should laugh at their mistakes or resort to shame and ridicule as punishment. Let me not tempt a child to lie or steal. So guide me hour by hour and day by day that I may demonstrate by all I say and do that honesty produces happiness.

Reduce, I pray, the meanness in me. May I cease to nag and when I am out of sorts, Oh Lord, to hold my tongue. Give me a ready word for honest praise.

Allow me not to rob them of the opportunity to grow up into responsible human beings, the desire to wait on themselves, to think, to choose and to make their own decisions.

Make me fair and just and loving. Help me to be considerate and compassionate and a companion to my children... to the point that they will have genuine esteem for me. Fit me to be loved and imitated by my children. Oh, God, please give me calm and poise and self-control in all of my life situations. Help me to be like your Son in attitude and love so that my children will also be like your Son in their life choices and actions.

AMEN